Property of
The Artists Hand
Courtesy of
WORDS DANCE PUBLISHING

SparkleFat
Poems That Intend To Be Seen

by Melissa May

WORDS DANCE PUBLISHING
WordsDance.com

Copyright © Melissa May 2014

No part of this book may be used or performed without written consent from the author except for in critical articles & reviews.

1st Edition
ISBN-13: 978-0692225417
ISBN-10: 0692225412

Cover photo by Juli Bowen & adapted by Amanda Oaks
Proofread & edited by Amanda Oaks
Interior design by Amanda Oaks

Words Dance Publishing
WordsDance.com

SparkleFat
Melissa May

A Fatward from the Author. 3

Poems That Intend To Be Seen

Conversation with a Miracle Body. 7
Fat Girl. 8
Dear Ursula. 10
Letters from a Fat Woman to the World That Created Her. . . . 13
Belly. 16
Wherein I Supernaturally Detach from my Body and-. 18
Love Letter: A Triad of Solos. 20
To Girls Who Imagine Themselves More Ghost Than Flesh. . . . 22
The Magic- A Bedtime Story. 25
To the Strangers and the Not Strangers Who Continue to Use
the Word Fat Like a Weapon. 27
Mantra for a Body in Flux. 30
Manifesto of Reclaiming. 31
Love Letter – For the Symphony. 35
An Open Letter to Fat-Shamers from an Incendiary Body. 36
A Spell for Reclaiming Your Body. 39
Exorcism. 42
Funny. 44
Symphony. 47
Heavy. 50

★ ★ ★

A Big, Fat, Grateful Heart. 55

A Fatward from the Author

Hello – my name is Melissa and I am a human magpie. Or maybe I'm a raccoon, or an ostrich, or perhaps a lovable though easily-distracted gibbon – because I *really* like things that sparkle. There has been a deeply rooted love of sparkly things in me from a very young age. This led to wearing body glitter well into adulthood (come at me bro), owning clothing made of material I am certain cannot be legal in any country that honors the Geneva Convention, and the unavoidable awkward-freak-out-shit-look-away after being busted for staring adoringly at people wearing glam gear and shining their shiny shine shine. Being busted is never a big deal, though – people who wear sparkles like they just wrapped themselves in the Nuclear Fission of the Goddamn Milky Way are intentional about many things, and one of them is **being seen**.

I am not supposed to be seen. I am 5 feet 9 inches tall, I weigh somewhere in the floating range between 290 and 310 pounds, I have a not-traditionally celebrated figure (as in not the exaggerated feminine ideal up-sized to larger proportions). I have an ill-defined waist, back fat, a low-hung double belly (FUPA), almost no neck to speak of, smaller thighs with lots of loose skin, arguably fantastic calves attached crudely to my dad's gnarled hobbit feet, and the not-traditionally-classic though classic-to-my-maternal-genetic-code schnoz. I have crooked teeth and a big goofy nose and small weird-blue eyes. I am, what any doctor will tell you, MORBIDLY obese (I hate to all-caps that word, but that's how people always say it. Not morbidly obese, MORBIDLY obese. Like for real, yo. That shit is morbid.) I have been taught, from so many eager teachers (peers, adults, health-care professionals, strangers, boys and girls I loved from afar, well-intentioned 'friends', "secret" lovers and a culture focused on conventional beauty measurements) that there is nothing to be proud of about my body. My body is meant to be quiet, to be clothed in unassuming patterns and mute colors, to be shamed into corners and only accessed at the pity and convenience of others.

But I was not born for beige, my loves. And neither were you. My body intends to be seen.

> My body intends to shine. My fat is not quiet.
> **My fat sparkles.**

That's what you're holding, dear one. You're holding *SparkleFat*. You're holding a loud, unapologetic, intentional book of poetry about my body, about your body, about fat bodies and how they move through the world in every bit of their flash and spark and burst. Some of the poems are painful, some are raucous celebrations, some are reminders and love letters and quiet gifts back to the vessel that has traveled me so gracefully - some are a hymnal of yes, but all of them sparkle. All of them don't mind if you look – really. They built their own house of intention, and they draped that shit in lime green sequins. All of them intend to be seen. All of them have no more fucks to give about a world that wants them to be quiet.

So come with me. We'll get our sparkle on, together.

- Melissa

SparkleFat
Poems That Intend To Be Seen

Conversation with a Miracle Body

Once I told my body, "You slow sickness, you sum of too many parts, you heavy and insurmountable burden. How will anyone find you in this forest of shame, this circus of flesh? How can anyone love a mountain?"

Once I told my body, "You swollen apology. You wilting bud. You slow-leaking cloud. This is what you deserve. This is exactly what you deserve."

Once I told my body, "Of course he closes his eyes when he makes love to you. He has hung another version of your skin on the insides of his eyelids. He is waiting for you to crawl out of this shell to love you, eyes open."

Once I told my body, "You are not sexy. You are not shine. You are not spark, not tinder, not flash, not smoke. You are not gorgeous. Not naked. Not deserving. Not a body to be loved. You are not. You are not. You are not."

And my body answered, slow thunder voice, "I am. I will be. I always have been. Unashamed. Pink glow. Gorgeous intention. Hung low belly. Sweet high. Always open. Wrapped in this light. Beautiful. Unshakable. No apology. Sexy. Formed from worth. Soft as hope. Hard as forever. Strong enough to anchor this storm. Big enough for both our joy. I am. I am. I am."

Fat Girl

So the poet tells me, all cloaked in beautiful words and
authentic Albanian eyebrows
that she makes clothes for bodies,
not bodies for clothes.
My body sits folded in a wicker chair like
two pallets of rising dough.
I pray she can't see my navel tremble.

I tell her,
I have been the fat girl in over a dozen schools.
I sit all token-like in their hall of fame, except–
they don't give awards to punch lines.
So I repeat the code of conduct like a mantra, even years
after the cap and gown have yellowed in the Oklahoma sun.

Do not like boys.
Do not go for seconds.
Do not draw attention.

See I know what a body feels like when it changes from vessel
to funeral shrouds,
to sarcophagus.
I have been buried alive for so long,
I've forgotten what the sun
tastes like.

But they're allowed to hate me.
Even now, strangers on the street
are allowed their sharp-tongue judgment, their sound effects.
Being this big is fuel for the last appropriate hate crime.
It is stand-up acceptable in its pretty designer suit–
size medium, pressed in brand new shoes.

It's my fault.
I will never curve like a comma around the bodies
of people I am not allowed to love,
I'm supposed to settle for anyone who
can stomach my punctuation.

But, I can change.
Somewhere between crash diets
and elastic-waist-band-jeans
there is another body waiting to be carved from between my hips.
I swear if I find her, I will send her out in ambassador-advocate glory
while the rest of me stalks dark corners because you never forget
that black can be so
slimming.

There is no symphony that plays for fat girls.
We are tuba-beats.
There is no graceful exit when we leave this world.

I have tried taking my life twice, and would
have tried for number three,
if it weren't for the thought of my parents' embarrassment
when the firemen struggled to load me on the gurney.
God forbid they should post
the weight of their disappointment in my obituary.

Instead, my bathroom is a 6am showdown
where I remind the mirror with tethered words that
so many women are counting on me to be strong, because
if fat girls can convince themselves they are beautiful,
surely they can hold on until their bodies are grown, stretched
and slim.

There will never be a parade celebrating our independence.
We are only allowed to congregate around self-loathing
and new age diet fads.

I will never mourn the body I should have had.
I do not pity handfuls of flesh; my heart is spit-fire hot
and so ready to burn.

But I've been dodging words alone for over twenty years now,
so— it should come as no surprise
just how quickly
I can move
for my size.

In 2012, Disney released a line of villain dolls depicting Ursula, the classically full-figured Sea Witch from The Little Mermaid as a designer, couture, size zero.

Dear Ursula
A Letter of Condolence

From one rolling midsection and
tameless will to another, my sweet Ursula—
I cannot imagine, the sick flip
of your stomach,
to see your image dissected, chins shaved,
waist cinched,
your silhouette robbed of every ounce of
delicious curve.
To find after two decades of existence that
your evil was more worthy of preservation
than the iconic body that held you,
you – big lady, were the only Disney character
that ever looked like me.
And while you may not have had the
waist-line of a princess
I'll be goddamned if you didn't have
the swagger of a Queen.
The way you sashayed around your lair
in full makeup
black flamenco number cut
so low in the back that your
every twist and shimmy displayed
the gorgeous tuck of your rolls.
You made back-fat look
fucking ***sexy***.

You made living in this body
a little less
like a curse.

I wonder how they told you,
did they sit you down over tea, delicately
frosted cakes lining your chipped porcelain?

Explain it as a marketing technique,
a vehicle to make you more palatable to
a culture that demands perfection?
I hope you crushed the teapot in the
clench of your fist.
I hope you grew a hundred feet tall
and drowned them in the whirlpool of your rage.
I wish I could have watched you suck the voices
from their tiny, breakable throats.

But I know you wept.
I know you licked the icing from
each and every cake
I know you broke, like a slow burn.

Wasn't it enough that they
made you a witch?
That you were already beyond the
bounds of their franchise royalty?
They expected little girls to recoil from the
wicked inside your laugh,
when instead, they worshiped your
honesty.

Ursula,
I don't want you cut down into
bite-sized pieces.
You weren't easy to swallow
for a reason.
I want you larger than life,
flaming red lips,
black flamenco dress–
I want the thick of your
tentacles,
your conjurer's hands,
the jiggle of your ample bust.
I want you dressed to the nines
on a runway.
I want every little girl to see a heroine
in a size 24.

Ursula, Queen of the Ocean,
you were never just a witch to me.
You were perfect—
every pound,
every inch,
every swell, perfect.

And I *pity* the poor, unfortunate soul
who would dare paint you as
anything less.

12 Letters from a Fat Woman to the World That Created Her

Dear God:
Was the soul you pushed
past my petal lips so fragile, you
had to give me all of this
flesh to protect it?

Dear Mom:
Thank you for this backbone.
Thank you for the neck of
confrontation.
Thank you for telling me I was
beautiful before I ever needed
to hear it.

Dear Dad:
I know you wanted
me to be a knockout...
I am.

Dear Kindergarten Boyfriend:
I'm sorry the other boys laughed at you
when I kissed you behind the bookshelf—
I have learned to be so careful with
my kisses, now that I know
the damage just one
can do.

**Dear Doctors, Nurses, Lab Techs and Dietitians
who have tried to determine for so long
why it is that I'm fat:**
My thyroid is fine.
I'm sorry that my mother
yelled at you when you told her
there was nothing wrong with me.
It was the best tasting pill
I have ever swallowed.

Dear 9th Grade Gym Teacher:
Yes, I can do a real push-up—
no, it was not okay for you to stop
the dodge-ball game and let
the whole class watch me prove it.

Dear Obviously-Gay-High-School-Boyfriend:
I knew.
We all knew.
But it felt so good to walk down
the hall with your hand braided in
my own like a normal girl that
I just didn't care.

Dear Abnormally Beautiful Sister:
I am sorry for all the times the bitter
seed of envy churned in my stomach
while looking at you.
You are more than just your
body, too.

Dear Heather Bennett:
When you told our 4th grade class that
I weighed a thousand pounds, I wished
that you could be ugly like me.
When you were in a tragically disfiguring car
accident in middle school, I felt like I
clawed that scar across your cheek—
like I shortened one of your legs while you slept
and your limp was my masterpiece,
I celebrated.
I am so ashamed.

Dear Older Brother:
As it turns out, my name is not
Fatty Fat McGee.
The man who loves me has
given me a new name,
I came to him in a white dress,
I did not care that I was big and pale

like the moon.
In his eyes, I am infinite.

Dear Man Who Loves Me:
When you tell me I am beautiful,
and I drop my head,
do not let me.

When you walk proudly with me at
your side, and I cower,
do not let me.

When I try to leave, because this world
has convinced me that I do not deserve someone
as perfect and beautiful as you—

Do Not Let Me.

It will take a lifetime to relearn the
language of loving myself,
I will always want to give up—
do not let me.

Dear Self:

There is nothing wrong with you.
Not a single goddamn
thing.

Belly
A Love Song

Belly, not beauty.
Belly, not beauty.

Belly –
you deserve roses.
You deserve sonnets and balconies of
lovesick declarations.
You un-uglied duckling,
high-tide of miracle.
ripple-wave of womanhood,
this is for you.

Belly, beautiful.
Belly, beautiful.
Belly –
every fold, a mystery.
Every pale stretch and pucker,
every day spent in binding,
every sweet, soft moment written
into your giving flesh,
this is all for you.

Belly – not beauty.
Fuck that.
Belly – not beauty.
Yeah, but touch it.

There is nothing hard about you.
There is nothing but offering.
You, womb and protector,
cage of circulation,
miracle of vessels,
museum of scars,
this is all for you.
This is all for your glory.

Boy sees belly, an object running forward

through time, a death sentence future.
Girl sees belly, is a thankful church of relief.
Creator sees belly, knows it by name,
recognizes her stitch work,
has given breath to every lively inch of intestine,
knows the liver's in recovery,
loves every sweet, ticking morsel beneath the skin.
Loves it.
Loves it all.

Belly, not beauty –
beholder doesn't recognize.
Beholder declares majestic.
Neighboring appendages grow jealous
of the sashay of its fleshy curve,
of its full bottom lip,
of its cramp and release,
of its fullness.

Belly, this is for you.
Belly, you are beauty.

Belly, forgive me.

Forgive the fingers that have pulled you like taffy.
Forgive the fist that tried to choke you empty.
Forgive the years of praying for your slow destruction.

Belly, forgive the taunting in my own tongue,
for my eyes and their easy persuasion,
for feet that refuse to dance to a tune you can move with.

Thank you for the warmth,
for the honest dent of stretch mark,
for the cradle of life,
for the deep pit of navel.

Belly, beautiful.
Belly, Beautiful.

Wherein I Supernaturally Detach from My Body and Join In with the Crowd Stoning My Flesh for Its Fullness by Telling the Whole Story of Why I Have Always Been Unafraid to Fight

Let's blame her mother! I say. It all started in the toxic Eden of her womb, the twisted genetic splendor. Let's blame her confounded immune system and her wide hips and her faulty pancreas and her round after round of steroid use just to birth this pink seed turned oak turned weeping willow.

Let's blame her mother who always told her she was just as beautiful as the sun. And big. And unashamed. Let's blame her mother who told her she could be anything and then let her be everything. Let's blame her mother for the night upon night of weeping and the doubt and the sickness of spirit and that gorgeous brewpot backbone, no–

Let's blame her father! I scream. Let's blame her father for wanting her to be the woman his mother wasn't. Let's blame her father for shaming her because that is the only means of change ever offered to him! Let's blame her father for loving her mother's belly full of his children, for loving her second mother's body full of quiet and strength and work. For loving women round, for loving women wide, for sparking their flesh, marrying their thick. Let's blame her father for not knowing how to care for a daughter so goddamn wild she was forced to grow her own field of possibility. Let's blame her father for teaching her to love the muck and blood and gut of this world, for her affair of words, for her laughter, for the gore of her fight–

no, no...

Let's blame her brother! Her brother who stood at the bus stop and joined in with the other's taunting! Who would temper any accolade with "But you're fat, so who fucking cares." Who pitied her and hated her for her weakness, no!

Her sister! Her beautiful sister who only aged into her body so gorgeously. Who dated boys her sister only dare love in the dark.

Who was the most slender altar to burn her flesh in offering,

NO!

NO!

Let's blame her! Let's blame her for her fingerprints in the mashed potatoes (never-mind that those potatoes stopped her from filling her belly with pills, stopped her burning another trophy into her thigh, stopped the darkness from whispering her name). Let's blame her for her lack of self-control and her audacity to wear her skin so proudly. Let's blame her for the heap she has grown into. Let's blame her for the foul and evil way she does not break. Let's blame her for the stupid way she grins, so stupid, doesn't she know? Doesn't she know that she shouldn't be allowed to be loved so openly? Doesn't she know making love to her shadow will only bring more skin out of hiding?

Throw one stone for her proud breasts and another for her bright and blinding laughter

and another for the way she slips out of her
shame like a fan dance, hypnotic–
and throw and throw and throw and
bury it all down.
Stone and stone and stone and stone–
and look:

You have made a mountain.

You have made a mountain for
her to dance upon–
and the only person you have
to blame is
yourself.

Love Letter: A Triad of Solos

Dear Body,

This is my promise to you:
I will not make jokes at the expense of your flesh.
I will not be valued in spite of you.
I will not be valued because of the hell I can put you through.
You are no one's goddamned punchline.
You are not MY punchline.
You are not a topic of conversation at dinner parties.
You are not the quickest way to get a laugh.
I will not make you bastard. I will not make you expendable.
I will not use you as a shield for my tender heart.
I love you. You are worthy of love. If we laugh together, we do.
But never at you. Never at you. Never again AT you.

Dear Body,

When someone tells you that you are beautiful, say thank you. But do not let that gratitude grow legs in your belly that will immediately bend for them.

You are sexy. You are sex. You have sex. You are worthy of sex. When people look at you, they often have sexy thoughts. Sexy sex thoughts about the hard and soft bits of you, about the slick and wet of you. About the awesome power of your breasts and cunt and mouth. Everything about this is normal. You are attractive. The fact that your body is sexy, attractive, endearing, arousing, sensual, IS NO SURPRISE. The fact that people find it this way when they look at it IS NO SURPRISE. You don't have to give pieces of it away to people just for saying so.

Be Sexy Selective. Be Buxom Bombshell. Be Dame Dynamo. Just don't be surprised.

Dear Body,

Sometimes the brain that sings to you and whispers good words in your ears and sends you sweet electric puckers *is an asshole*.

Some days, you want to reach into the center of your mind and find the darkness your mother gave you – this manic wilderness that arrests your limbs and unhinges your reality – and rip that bleeding animal from your wet murky lobes. Some days, you just want to be able to look at your own reflection and not see her decay staring back at you.

You were given a strange and terrible gift; a box of old grief, a worry chest, a cracked mirror to see the world with. The person at the wheel of your mind is not always a friend. The thoughts you have about yourself will not always be kind. You will not always be able to love yourself the way you deserve to be loved.

Do not worry. You are not broken. The gift you've been given is truly a gift. This terrifying thing has taught you to recognize truth, to look into the mouth of fear and know, to call it out in a crowd and speak light into your flesh when its darkness is a lie.

To Girls Who Imagine Themselves More Ghost than Flesh

I see you.
Pressed into the high-gloss
shine of wooden floors,
peeking out from the bright squint
of windowpanes, tucked neatly
into the towels in the hall closet – watching.
Your skin does not blend
into the backdrop of mahogany
quite the way you had imagined.
I can tell you planned to zip invisible
through doors, under carpets, into the banister
rounded like your mother's hip.
This place you built to hold your haunt
is home to all of your fear.
You just needed a place to come
when your body became too heavy.
I know that weight,
but ghosts are never truly ghosts
until there is someone living
to mourn them, and the only thing you are
haunting is your own
weary skin.

Love, you will never spirit
into a room where you are wanted
and leave any less solid.
It is an impossible thing, to
truly be unseen.
To be chill and
dark and un-mattered
in a home that is really a home.

This house you have built
is held together with untruths.
The walls are hung with the pictures
of love that you have lost,

love that is gone from you now.
The people smiling from their glossy frames
whisper that you will never again know
the warmth of them, that death is the end
and they are dead now.
The floors are built from
the bedrooms of all the places
you have ever felt safe.
They are studded with nails and glass
and the sharp edges of dangerous things.
You cannot even lay against them
to remember without bleeding.
All that was safe will pierce you.
There is no safety here,
so you love things that are wounded.
Things that are hungry.
You build this love a house and
you convince yourself that it is
enough to hold you.
That its sharp and waiting mouth is
strong enough to make you disappear.

But I see you.
I see your past encrypted
into your arms.
I see the shame that
drives your groaning feet
I see you, crumpling yourself,

folding in on your own limbs.
But you are not invisible.
You are no ghost.
The door, my love
it is built from the hands
of women who have found
their way out.
We have all grown mirror
in anticipation of your exit.
We are waiting for you,

to see you
exactly as we do.

Love, we are waiting
for you
to **see**.

The Magic– A Bedtime Story

Sweet fat body, as I tuck you snug into your big cushion bed, as I kiss your sweet plump pumpkin cheeks, as I zip you warm into this skin all your own, as I nuzzle the soft belly of your chin and wrap our arms around our arms because our arms are big enough to cradle entire tiny universes between their plush, I want to sing you the sweetest pie-crust song. But I cannot sing - so I'll write you a story instead.

In this story, you are exactly you. You are not shaved down to proportions more easily swallowed by tight-throat scavengers. You are hero/heroine large and that is large enough for whatever body follows you into sleep. You are not some other body dreamed of.

In this story you are minding your own business doing nothing out of the ordinary. You are planting cucumbers in your backyard garden, you are shopping for new earrings to compliment the fluff of your perfect cheeks, you are drinking crisp wine and eating warm and creamy things in an outdoor cafe surrounded by all the good light - whatever. You're doing things. Imagine anything. Imagine everything.

In this story, people are walking by as people do. It's your dream, so you can imagine the people however you want, sweet body. You can imagine they are made of erector sets and carrot tops, you can imagine their legs are really smiley sharks that have politely swallowed their feet so they are slip-sliding around the streets all gummy and full of song. Or they can just be people. Just regular old gorgeous folk.

In this story, they are catching glimpses of your big fat body. They are passing you glances like notes in social studies, grade 8. They are brushing by you in store aisles; they are walking their dogs down your alley and getting an eye-full of your shorty-short-wrapped thighs.

And they say nothing. And they smile. And they think quietly to themselves, *what a normal person, what a gorgeous breathing soul, what adorable shorts, what a blinding song that person is.* They offer to buy you a drink. They inquire about all that bloom in your garden. They pick up a pair of brave earrings and say, *here, I think these would make your sweet, kind face look extra shiny today.*

In this story, the word fat doesn't barb up in their mouths. You are SparkleFat and everyone loves you. They don't have the slightest inclination to scoff. They don't whisper to their neighbors or lamp posts or brooches anything about your health.

In this story, you are seen for exactly what you are – a person. A beautiful, complicated, faceted, extraordinary person. You are not invisible and you are not fetish and you are not less than and you are not worst-case-scenario and you are not other. In this story, you are gorgeously you. Exactly as you are.

And you know the best thing about dreams, sweet fat body? They can be real. They can be real the second someone gives them legs to walk.

To the Strangers and the Not Strangers Who Continue to Use the Word Fat Like a Weapon
A Linguistics Lesson

A simple scan through the latest edition
of Webster's Dictionary will yield more than
20 definitions for the word *fat*.
The majority of these definitions are adjectives –
descriptive words used to modify a noun.
Fat can also be a noun.
The origin of the word *fat* predates
the year 1000, from Latin to Germanic
to Old English to Middle English,
nearly every variation of tongue claims a hold
on the word 'fat'.
Its original definition meant 'to stuff or cram'.
The first definition listed under the word *fat*
means obese, corpulent, or having too much tissue.
The definitions beneath that mean plentiful, abundant
profitable, wealthy, affording in good opportunities –
funny, the way our culture ostracizes the *too much*
when it is inconvenient and seeks it out
when it is beneficial.
The way we whittle words into weapons
and hurl them at the soft flesh of whatever it is
that we fear–

but fat is not a bullet.
Fat is not a consequence,
is not an insult, is not a
state of mind, is not an open platform
for your opinion.
Fat is not lazy.
Fat does not mean unhealthy,
does not mean diabetes,
does not mean high blood pressure,
does not mean heart attack.
Fat is not a death sentence.
Fat is not a matter of control.
Fat is not ugly,

is not disgusting, is not shameful,
is not a weakness.
Fat is not a thing to be warned against.
Is not a worst case scenario.
Is not the most terrible thing
that can happen to you or someone
you love.
Fat does not mean dieting, does
not mean unhappy, does not mean
desperate to be thin.
Fat does not mean *help me!*
Fat is not a thing to be fixed, is not
a corner to shove your displaced concern.
Fat is not your fucking business when it
belongs to someone else.

Fat is an adjective.
Is a word.
Is three letters.
Who knew it could hold
so much weight?

I know what fat is.
It is the body, not the cross that I carry,
and you cannot have it anymore.
I am taking fat back.
I am putting it on the highest of
high shelves, I am tending to its broken
and bloody and misused.
I am spooning nourishment past its lips.
I am giving fat its life back.

You have already tried to steal the ability
to love my body in all of its fullness,
you will not pull the heaviness of language
from my mouth as well.

But yes, since you took the time to
point it out, I am fat.

I am not ashamed.
I am not shamed.
I am not revolting.
I am not silenced.
I am not going anywhere.
I take up space.
I take up space that I deserve.

Yes. I am fat.
Fuck you very much
for noticing.

Mantra for a Body in Flux

Dear Muddled Heartbeat,
   Dear Tired Spine,
      Dear Asymmetric Hips,
         Dear Body,

            You have no excuse to give up.
            You have no excuse to give up.

Dear Willful Curls,
   Dear Blackened Lungs,
      Dear Cavern Pores,
         Dear Skin,

            You were born before you believed in broken.
            You were born before you believed in broken.

Dear Timid Womb,
   Dear Lacerated Spirit,
      Dear Silent Throat,
         Dear Overworked Tongue,

            You are a song worth singing.
            You are a song worth singing.

Manifesto of Reclaiming
For M.J.

All of my failings, gather, lean in,
and feast upon the glory of
your undoing.

Gorge yourself thick as August
plums on my defeat.
This is the moment when your
triumph no longer diminishes the
hot and bright of me.

No longer swallows me up in
the brittle of your hands until
the only skin is my skin and the
only pain is my pain and the
only love is the love hard fought and
slowly diminishing -
the love that I do not deserve,
the love that I do not have.

This is the undiminishing of me.

A call to all of my magical mistakes,
you are welcome here.

Unpack your bones and throw them
sloppy on couches.
Be unmoving in the presence of
new hearts, do not hide your rot.
You are the framework that holds me,
broken is not a thing to
be fixed, it is an opening
to make room and there is so
much room in these bones.

A call to all of the bones,
I will open for you,
will be calm in all of the

dirt and fuckup and uncomfortable pauses
where I am growing to accommodate
your gorgeous stretch.
I reclaim every second I lived in fear
of this breaking.

A call to the unbest self that hides
her tangled corners and cannot part her
hair and laughs too much and
never learned to coordinate her shoes and
says things that should not be said and
is complacent.
Unbest self, you are
welcome here – come
out from behind that smile.
Be free in your unknowing.
Be freed on your awkward angles
and the slick stares of people you
worship like suns.
Have you smelled the God in you today?
It smells like crabgrass and
spring and your mama's hands and
there are gods in you today.
There are gods in you every day.
I reclaim this tower of soiled flesh.
I reclaim this holy.

A call to bodies,
a call to lovers,
a call to every popping cell and
glittering electron that makes the
muck of loving so worth it.
Bodies, you are welcome here.
Bodies, you are welcome to unthread
and be glow in this, a space shaped
in the shape of you.
Loosed is your finite and your
reforming and your transient fullness.
Loosed is every drip of shame.
I reclaim all the love I have birthed

like children into the forest
of my shame.
I reclaim the timbre of those branches.
I make a new space to love these
bodies bold and nude and full.

A call to circumstance,
I own this moment,
I own this moment and this
moment is welcome here.
This unmoving, this brazen, this
happening is what I will make of it.
This happening is my own.
This conjuring, mine.
I reclaim all that I have allowed to
happen to me,
I will happen for *me*.

A call to the future –
come ready.
Come promising sweet and impossible
things, come with full hands, come with
all of your apprehension.
Come open road and imaginary and
filled with a fool's hope.
Fools, you are welcome here.
Get stupid and drunk on your
own unknown.
Flip backlash, fuck freefall.
Twirl in a bell-bottomed dress
until you fall sick and vomit up
your indecision – it's okay.
There is enough terror to go around
but that dress is not
going to twirl itself and our
feet will not bravely walk toward what
we do not know forever.
So while we are young, we will walk
I erase the name of
my story because it is not finished.

I reclaim this path in the name
of what will be.

A call to the wilderness,
a call to the hunger of beasts,
(namely my own).

Here is all that I am.

Here is every hurt, every failing
every gorgeous mistake.
Here is my naked flesh.
Here is my shame.
Here is my brave unknowing.
Here is my happening.
Here is me.
There is nothing left to envy, no
joy remaining in the hunt of my weakness.
I take it all back.
I take it all.
I reclaim it.
There is not a shred of regret to
fill your belly on.
I own everything that has
happened, that will happen,
I own my happening.
I reclaim the joy of my simple flesh.
May you rot, thick August plum,
on the branch -
this forest is mine.

Love Letter– For the Symphony

Dear Other Bodies,

I have coveted you. I have worn my flesh in war against you. I have prayed to never end up like you. I have prayed to go back in time and steal the song from your perfect lungs. I have wished you sickness. I have held you responsible for my own imperfect love. I have ravaged you with teeth so dull it almost felt like a whisper. I have let comparison steal the joy I should have given you space for. I have mocked you. I have made my husband say I am more beautiful than you. I have hated you. I have made you an object. I have made you a prayer. I have made you a river I am grateful I do not have to swim in.

I am sorry for the long history of war, stealth, and secret. I am sorry that I have looked at a body and removed it of the humanity inside. I'm sorry that I have taken a hammer to any body shaped like a more attractive nail. I am sorry for not loving you the way I have loved myself. I am sorry for being angry that you do not have to walk this road. I am sorry for the language of envy burned into my tongue.

Dear Other Bodies – please know, when I fall madly in love with myself, I am falling madly in love with you as well. I am undoing all of the education about how to love these vessels. I am learning a new language of freckle and pock and open.

Dear Other Bodies – my body is not always a light house. But when I am dangerous for you to travel near, I will not climb the rocks of my own insecurity and siren you into the cliffs. I will not make you a meal to feed my own emptiness. I will not punish my skin by comparison. I will not let envy steal my joy. I will not treat any body like an escape hatch out of my own responsibility. I will hold you as fully and completely as I hold myself: in accountability, in grace, and in truth.

Signed,
A body –
a perfectly flawed body.

An Open Letter to Fat-Shamers from an Incendiary Body

**I was not born knowing how to hate this body.
I learned.**

Lesson 1 – *Because I am fat, I am not wanted.*

Last night, I held a terrified child in my arms, careful of her bruises.
This is my job.
I am round like her mother, and so she clung to my
flesh looking for a piece of home.
Before she fell asleep, she pinched my face between
her pink hands and
told me she was so glad I was fat.
She knew she'd be safe then.
She nestled her head against my shoulder.
She slept all night.

Lesson 2 – *If I could just exercise some control, I could be un-fat.*

The night my father spit in my mother's face 8 times and busted
open her lip.
The night my mother went, finally, insane.
The night my mother tried to fuck another mental patient in the
courtyard during visiting hours.
The night my mother tried to set our house on fire while we slept.
The night my mother fucked her dealer while I feigned sleep
on the futon.
The night my father chose everyone else but me.
The night my father chose everyone else but me.
The night my father chose everyone else but me.
The first night my mother didn't come home.
The third night my mother didn't come home.
The night my father told me he'd kill himself in front of me
if I didn't go away.
The night my father told me he wanted to wire my jaw shut.
The night my mother slept while the man found my bedroom door.
The night she told me if it even happened at all, it happened
because I wanted it.
All the nights I never learned to cope any other way.

Lesson 3 – *Because I am fat, no one will ever love me.*

The night of my 18th birthday, after we returned
from the strip club, I sucked my
neighbors dick while he watched TV over my
bobbing head.
I cried myself to sleep, not out of shame -
but out of gratitude that someone finally
wanted me.

Lesson 4 – *Because I am fat, I am ugly.*

When my husband tells me that I am beautiful,
your voice is the only goddamn thing I can hear.
I make him say it so often, he grew a
pull cord from the base of his spine.
When I pull it, I daydream of him with thin, beautiful women.

Lesson 5 – *I am so fat, I should just kill myself*

When I was 11, with Tylenol. I left a note. I woke up.
When I was 16, with nitroglycerin tablets. I didn't leave a note.
I woke up.
Prom night. He only danced with me once, I burned 17 corsages
into my thigh.
A scar for each one of your chuckles.
Every day in between.
Every day after.

Lesson 6 – *I'm so fat, I'm going to die of a heart attack*

The first time I looked at my body naked in the mirror, I mean
really looked at it. Touched it. Made love to myself.
Invited the world in. Unfolded.
My heart swelled so much it nearly burst.
My body knows what it feels like to be attacked, but
this did not feel like war.

Lesson 7 – *Because I am fat, I am stupid and lazy.*

I learned to operate all of your weapons with better accuracy.
I learned all the words to my own eulogy.
I learned more danger than your mouth is capable of holding.
I learned to fill myself on hatred for this body without the smug satisfaction chaser.
I learned to swallow it all down.
I learned to swallow it all down.
I learned to unravel into the most deserving whipping post.
I learned it all.

Lesson 8 – *I unlearned.*

Lesson 9 – *I am still waiting for you to catch up.*

A Spell for Reclaiming Your Body
After Mindy Netifee

I.
There are no outside ingredients,
you already have what you need
bubbling away inside of you.
You are the cupboard where your
magic is kept, forgotten now.
Dust off the mortar,
unhinge the pestle from the back
of the junk drawer,
get all your tools together
and get ready to pluck.
Things may have shifted around inside the
bright cavern of your chest, but
it's all there:

- Eye of Body Dysmorphic Disorder
- Tongue of Quiet, Respectable Woman
- Hair of Wildness, Tamed
- The Liver of One-Too-Many Boxes of Sunset Blush
- Belly, Thighs, Arm-Flap

Blessed Be.

II.
Sometimes, it's easier to pretend
that you never knew magic in the first place.

It's okay, this fear
I mean, they did burn women on pyres of
suspicion for much less than this.
Maybe that's why you put your conjure away.
Stashed you rhythmic tongue all the way
back in the freezer.
Trimmed down the broom bristles.
Tried to soothe yourself into the slender
of an agreeable woman.

You are not an agreeable woman.

You could be discovered.
You will be discovered.
You are being discovered.

That's the thing,
somewhere, you were convinced that
the curve of your hat was too much.
That you needed to tone down your cauldron,
trade it for a Dutch oven.
Trade it for certain kind of acceptance.
Trade it for your power.
Your powers.

III.
Fat is not a four letter word.

Bitch is along those lines, but it only
falls out of the mouths of
envy.

Of fear—
you used to clothe yourself in its
long, spindly fingers,
used to dress it in robes and fly it
across the midnight of so many unsuspecting lovers,
used to chant to the hollow
of its intended wound.

You can borrow my tongue if you need to.
You can take off your clothes and
just be naked in this moment,
in your reclaiming,
in your re-witching hour.
You can find a photograph of yourself
in the days of your majestic.
Tuck it neatly between your thighs.

Bleed heavy and slow until
that woman is revived.
Until she has breath.

You can throw all the quiet you've swallowed
into the hot bubble of this iron pot.
Watch the need to reshape yourself melt
in the smoke.
Watch the ticking of your internal clock
dissolve back into ghost.
Watch your spine retwist into
backbone under the wave of its
wicked flame.

IV.
The first day your power returns, you
will still drink wine.
You will sit alone in your bed and weep
for the safety of your predictable life, for your
bitten tongue.
But know this–
This harness used to be familiar.
This coven is a witch mob.
This life requires more than your
silence to bleed.

You don't need anyone to read
you the instructions.

You have everything this spell will take:

- Your Bitch Throat
- Your Untamable Power
- Your Salty, Powdered Tongue

You were always magic.

So start the fire already.

Exorcism
In response to the question, 'Why do you continue to do this if it hurts so much?'

This is not a poem.
I am writing as though it were –
but it's just illusion,
a trick of the light.
The swirling darkness that nests
itself in my bones does not know
that this spell is its undoing.
It pounds its fists against the stage
and hungers for my weaknesses exposed,
demands to stick its fingers into my wounds–
because it does not know.

This is the way I make magic.
This is the way I give the darkness a name.
When I write of it – this cavity of me,
this rotting thing, when I say it out loud
in front of strangers, when I say it,
when I finally gather the strength,
it is not to elicit sympathy from the curious.

Not when I talk about the pills, or the days
of not showering, or the terrifying fits
of self-injury that felt like lighthouses
in a sea of locked doors.

Not to demonize the ones who made me believe
my own body would be best kept in death
where it can disappoint no one.
It's to say it is not smoke, this thing.
Not trapped in metaphor,
not unknown.
It is to say there is a name for it, a reckoning.
That I am not a beautiful tragedy, a comedy of juxtaposition.
It is an illness, but I am not my illness.
Not the embodiment of suffering.
I am not my poems.
So I say them

because when I say them,
they are no longer
phantom, no longer
quietly scratching nothingness.
No longer fear.
No longer nameless.
No longer powerful.
I am powerful.
Because I will not hide from my brokenness.
Will not mold myself into apology.
Will not ask permission
because I have never
found a place where my body
would be best kept in its nothing.
This is not a poem,
it is an exorcism.
This is how I call
the demon by its name:
Fear.
Depression.
Dysmorphia.
Hurt.
Mania.
Anxiety.
Shame.
Grief.
Shame.
Grief.
Shame.
Shame.
Shame.

This is how I warn the shadows
that the only one who names me –
Is **Me**.

Funny
After Robbie Q. Telfer

My mom loves when I visit home
Because you're so funny, she tells me,
and sometimes, she just needs to laugh.
My mom is married to a man half-perfect-smile,
half-whiskey-bottle.
She's got three adult children who get
stupid on their brave, and a
19 year old deployed in Afghanistan.
So sometimes, she really does need to laugh -
and I am happy to play that role for her.
It slides on familiar, this One-Act of Bravado
This Fools' Smile, This Idiot Parade,
And even when I am not feeling particularly
humorous, I still put on the costume
because everyone loves a funny girl.

It doesn't start this way, this is
what it becomes.
Born of armor, an escape hatch
of sharp tongues.
It started in 5th grade, when my
father wanted to wire my jaw shut
for an entire school year,
convinced I'd laugh a little more
if I could stop swallowing punchlines and
fill myself instead on the quiet comfort of fitting in.
They say kids are mean – they're not,
they're honest
and curious.
Adults are mean.
So I whittled these bones into a tower,
developed a whip-crack sense of
humor,
a sparkling personality,
taught myself funny.
Taught myself to laugh
a little more.

I've been laughing for 14 years.

By now, there is nothing that could be said
to puncture these interior walls.
I have sharp and gleaming comebacks for the
commentary of strangers.
I can make myself so small, no one would be
tempted to squash out this light.
I will cut myself first, distract
you with the blood.
I practice in the mirror.
Repeat every horrible insult with
painful clarity until my heart is
a still ocean.
Until I am uncrackable.
Until I am joyful under the
weight of it.

And when my mom needs to laugh,
I go back to that place,
to 9th grade biology,
the lab is cold and sterile and black as
my jester's tongue.
The boy two rows over screeches out a
loud **BOOM** every time my foot
meets the floor.
I whip my head around,
Godzilla my body and say,
It's a good thing there
were no Japanese Cities
between here and my chair,
otherwise – those poor bastards
would be toast!
Everyone laughs.
The boy never makes the **BOOM**ing sounds again.
I have stolen every bit of his
delicious fun.

But for the rest of my life, I will have to remember
that the only person who ever made me a
Monster
was Me.

Isn't it funny?
Isn't is so, so funny?

Symphony

This is my body.
Not a fumbling mass of flesh
and limb.
It is a concert hall.
An Orchestra –
Philharmonic-Erectus.
The liver is a low-sliding trombone.
Sounds like jazz and Creole coast line
smells like Bourbon Street.
Can no longer properly
filter out the bad notes.
Lets sour music infect the blood stream.
Chest cavity – wind section,
left lung flute and nicotine
right lung clarinet and Albuterol dependence.
They struggle with timing, can barely
catch their breath between songs.
Pancreas, contrabassoon,
lowest instrument in the entire orchestra.
Reaches so far down on the clef that is it felt,
rather than heard,
in your teeth, your fingertips,
felt in your fingertips, when it forgets the music
that is where it is felt.
Blood drawn, tested,
insulin injections are the only instruments that
will ever pick up its harmony.
Nerves – kettle drum, bass drum, cymbal snare.
They snap and fire under too much pressure.
They are untuned and wild and insistent.
The nervous system houses the maestro who
has lost control of his musicians.

Heart, first violin.
Nothing plays without its count
when it stops, there is no more music.

There are no bad instruments.

Only careless composers.
When the doctors said Diabetes,
High Blood Pressure,
Asthma, Inflamed Liver
Repressed Immune System
High Risk of Stroke and Heart Attack,
I realized, I was holding the pen,
It was the first time I asked God to take this away,
make me anything but a writer.
It is a hard truth, to stand guilty in
the mirror and face the empty opera boxes,
the naked stage of belly,
to realize you were given to this world in
all the right keys,
now rusted, sharp,
tone deaf,
so you learn a new song
before there is nothing left inside of you
but silence.

485 pounds, a funeral march,
the grave is a trumpet's swell of home.
412 pounds, my stomach picks up the growl
of bass line,
I learn to love the hollow thrum of percussion.
380 pounds, I fire the high-hats in my knees,
Let them know their crash and ricochet
are no longer required here.
385 pounds, I do not give up when the strings break.
379 pounds, I do not give up when I restring.
This is not for the instruments, this is for the Symphony.
320 pounds, my pancreas reclaims its solo, but
I can't feel it anymore.
My fingertips heal.

292 pounds,

   people still gawk at my warm-up,
   hold their ears at my crescendo

but I play loud,
sign every note with my progress.
I have sold tickets to concerts I will not play for
another fifty years,
but as God as my witness –
I **will** be there to
play them.

Heavy

My dad won't call me fat. Not to my face.
It's a small thing I've noticed, his quiet protection of me.
As though the word will call down some ancient curse,
write our history in blood, unravel us into otherness –
as if it were a secret.
When my body becomes predictable dinner conversation,
I watch him dance around the word with such familiar grace
until he settles – relieved,
upon its kind and unobtrusive neighbor.
Heavy, he calls me.
You're just **heavy**, princess.
Just a little heavy.

And I've decided that he's right.
I am feeling heavy these days.
I am heavy, lead-bodied girl.
Carry all my weight in my expectations.
Have hips wide as hope.
Today the scale said I weighed 8,922 pounds
and all but 297 of that is my heart.
But after a lifetime of carrying both the pity, and
the hatred, of strangers simultaneously,
carry well-meaning euphemisms,
carry the prayer of my own diminishing,
carry grief etched into the pink pucker of guilt,
I think it's time to hand some of this back.
Give the world its wish of my body.
Un-heavy myself.

First, take this shame.
It does not match this sapling pride, thirsty
for sunlight. Neither does it match my pink bikini,
my naked glory, or all of this goddamned audacity.

Take every time someone has told me *"you look like you've lost weight"*
as if they were saying *"you are finally becoming beautiful."*

You cannot have my ass. **My ass is perfect.**

But you *can* take the excuses given to my female lovers, their
confused faces as I explained why they could not kiss me there,
there where I am afraid, could not suck or swirl or taste me.
You can have all the moments I denied myself their love.

Take every bus bench. Take each airline seat – two at a time.
Take the stares in the mall. Take stairs. Take every gawk.
Take spanx. Take girdle. Take shaper.
Take collapsed organs and rash and scar for the sake of holding in.
Take the boom boom boom of stranger's unwelcome sound effects.
Take strangers. Take easy target. Take for your own good.
Take YouTube comments. Take anonymous. Take responsibility.
Take this ache in me, you can have it –
every day I monstered myself into a punchline
each time I called my body a broken symphony,
an untuned orchestra.
How silly, letting someone else tell me what kind of music my
body is supposed to make.

Please, take these tears. I do not need them anymore.
Take these iron excuses. This mountain of justifications.
Take all of your thinly veiled health concern and shove it up
your assumptions.

I would offer you myself, in whole. But I know what you would
do with this gorgeous stomach. This stunning double chin.
I know your designs for my brazen outward sprawl, and besides-
I have already given **enough**.
Too many years of hiding. Too many scars
Too many times I – thank God, mercifully – woke up.

It is the most excruciating irony – to be looked at constantly
but never really seen.
But here you are – seeing me. **So see me.**
See my feet, how they aren't even touching the ground –
they never were.
See me balloon, see me rise, see me wish-come-true
See me shed, and shed, and shed, and shed.
See how high this heavy, heavy girl
can fly.

51

Melissa May is a Youth-In-Crisis worker, body positivity/body justice activist, cat-call devourer, general unraveler of the patriarchy and salty feminist sass-mouth from Oklahoma. She has been a competitive spoken word artist since 2008, and has been both a multi-time Women of the World Poetry Slam finalist as well as the 3rd ranked poet in the world at the Individual Poetry Slam in 2012.

She has a degree in Youth Ministry and Bible and Theology that she is aggressively not using, is married to a mad scientist, loves harder than medically recommended, cannot physically stop cursing and smuggles thousands of secrets around like the precious and delicate things that they are. The only secrets she can't seem to keep are her own. That's what you're holding now. The un-doing of all her shame. The most rare and wild jewel of her heart. Smuggle it around real good. Keep it safe. She'll owe you big.

She knows you are perfect.

A Big, Fat, Grateful Heart

Anyone who has ever embarked on the path toward loving themselves can tell you – firmly – two things. 1 – It is a looooong journey. There is no quick fix. It is a lifetime of lessons. 2 – There is no way you can possibly get there alone. I have had an army of light in my life, fierce and loving humans who have fought with me and fought for me when my fists were too heavy to swing anymore. I want to recognize the people who have loved and held me so well. The sparkliest of loves.

First, to the warriors who paved this path before me – thank you. To every human who has ever looked at their body and seen it for the miracle thing that it is – thank you. To every person who ever told me to love my body exactly as it was – thank you. To Denise Jolly, who is so astoundingly brave with the way she loves herself in the open, who invited me on a journey to love my body that made this book a reality. Thank you. To Sonya Renee Taylor (creator of The Body Is Not An Apology) who forged a movement focused on inclusion and love that has saved my life over and over again – thank you. To Rachel Wiley – who speaks the language my heart speaks and who says all the words that make this body believe in home again. Thank you. To Lauren Zuniga, who convinced me to stay, in more ways than I can ever say. Thank you. To Desiree Dallagiacomo, who can make you laugh yourself out of your body and then lure you back in with all the gorgeous ways we learn how to heal. Thank you. These women embody everything about unapology, about love, about the divine skin and the freedom of acceptance. Thank you.

Next, to my community – thank you to every member of Red Dirt Home for Wayward Poets. Thank you for tender and often frustrating way you have grown me. Thank you for every time you clapped for poems that weren't all that good, cheered me on in my successes, held me in my failures, DAMN-ed me into confidence, and broke me open with your unflinching light. I am grateful for you in every way.

To my mother, who passed away February 17th, 2014. You were the first fat woman I ever loved. You were the first person who ever told me it was okay to love myself. For all the ways you sparked strength in me – thank you.

To my mom and dad – who accused me of plagiarizing the first poem I ever wrote – thank you. I know we joke about that day, and you jest that you'll never be able to live it down, but I'm grateful for it. Your first lesson was that one poem was never going to be enough to change anyone's mind; in that, I have always found the courage to write another. I can't wait to keep astounding and horrifying you with all the weird and wonderful words that pop out of my brain.

To my family – thank you for the nearly endless fountain of writing material.

Thank you to JULI BOWEN, who shot my body celebration session from which this book's cover picture was taken, and who is probably the most gentle and beautiful and truly good person I have ever met. Thank you to CHALYN BASSETT, who did my hair and makeup for the pictures, and who is the most alive and present friend a girl could ask for. I love you both so much.

Thank you to my two oldest friends, Sarah Morrow and Nethia White. You hold all this crazy and make it look effortless. You take such good care of this wild heart. Forever. I mean it.

A HUGE thank you to the staff at Words Dance Publishing and especially to Amanda Oaks, who made the daunting process of this book so stress-less and gorgeous. Amanda, I love you. I am thankful every day for you. Thank you for the ass-busting you do to make other writers feel like they deserve all the beauty you hand them.

Thank you to Jennifer-Leigh Oprihory and William James from TiredHearts Press, who allowed us to use "Fat Girl", "Dear Ursula", "Symphony", and "Funny" from my forthcoming manuscript, *Swallow the W i l d*, in this book. Thank you for believing in my art before I knew how to. #teamtomatoes

Thank you to Button Poetry (and Upworthy!) for featuring the video of "Dear Ursula" that reached so many people who needed to hear that they were not alone.

To my overnight co-worker Shawnda Baumann who has to sit and listen to me philosophize at 4AM and who also listens to every (sometimes really, really bad) poem I write in the middle of the night and who also has agreed and will forever uphold the "If one of us dies at work the other has to pluck their fallen comrade's face before the medics arrive" pact – bless you for not calling the authorities yet. I adore you.

To Mary Pinkoski, my little moon. The tenderness of your love is one of my most treasured gifts.

To my husband Caylon, who (mostly) does not understand me but resolves to love me through the perpetual storm of ALL THE FEELINGS ALL THE TIME – I love you. Thank you for always being my baseline, for teaching me home, for holding me in all seasons. The way you love me without question gives me the courage to love myself in the same way. If I sparkle at all, it is because your light always hits me just right.

To my big fat ass and my stunning FUPA and my thick thighs and my second chin and my weird hair and my crooked teeth and my round stomach and my soft skin and my gorgeous breasts and my perfect cunt and my present and easily accessible g-spot and my brave nose and my unending and unending and unending heart. Thank you body. Thank you.

And Finally - thank you to every person who has stopped apologizing for the space their bodies take up. Thank you for every imperfect miracle walking this earth right now, for every beautiful one of you. You take up all that space. You take up every last inch. You Shine. You Sparkle. You Light. You fucking deserve it.

Other titles available from
WORDS DANCE PUBLISHING

WHAT WE BURIED
Poetry by Caitlyn Siehl

| $12 | 64 pages | 5.5" x 8.5" | softcover |

ISBN: 978-0615985862

This book is a cemetery of truths buried alive. The light draws you in where you will find Caitlyn there digging. When you get close enough, she'll lean in & whisper, *Baby, buried things will surface no matter what, get to them before they get to you first.* Her unbounded love will propel you to pick up a shovel & help— even though the only thing you want to do is kiss her lips, kiss her hands, kiss every one of her stretch marks & the fire that is raging in pit of her stomach. She'll see your eyes made of devour & sadness, she'll hug you & say, *Baby, if you eat me alive, I will cut my way out of your stomach. Don't let this be your funeral. Teach yourself to navigate the wound.*

"It takes a true poet to write of love and desire in a way that manages to surprise and excite. Caitlyn Siehl does this in poem after poem and makes it seem effortless. Her work shines with a richness of language and basks in images that continue to delight and astound with multiple readings. *What We Buried* is a treasure from cover to cover."

— **WILLIAM TAYLOR JR.**
Author of *An Age of Monsters*

Other titles available from
WORDS DANCE PUBLISHING

LITERARY SEXTS

A Collection of Short & Sexy Love Poems
(Volume 1)

| $12 | 42 pages | 5.5" x 8.5" | softcover |

ISBN: 978-0615959726

HIT #1 ON AMAZON'S HOT NEW RELEASE LIST!

Literary Sexts is a modern day anthology of short love poems with subtle erotic undertones edited by Amanda Oaks & Caitlyn Siehl. Hovering around 50 contributors & 124 poems, this book reads is like one long & very intense conversation between two lovers. It's absolutely breathtaking. These are poems that you would text to your lover. Poems that you would slip into a back pocket, suitcase, wallet or purse on the sly. Poems that you would write on slips of paper & stick under your crush's windshield wiper. Poems that you would write on a Post-it note & leave on the bathroom mirror.

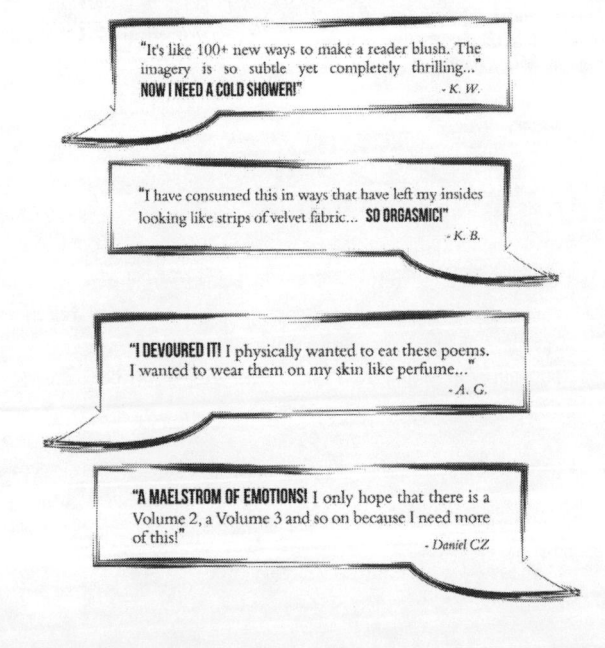

"It's like 100+ new ways to make a reader blush. The imagery is so subtle yet completely thrilling... **NOW I NEED A COLD SHOWER!**"
— *K. W.*

"I have consumed this in ways that have left my insides looking like strips of velvet fabric... **SO ORGASMIC!**"
— *K. B.*

"**I DEVOURED IT!** I physically wanted to eat these poems. I wanted to wear them on my skin like perfume..."
— *A. G.*

"**A MAELSTROM OF EMOTIONS!** I only hope that there is a Volume 2, a Volume 3 and so on because I need more of this!"
— *Daniel CZ*

Other titles available from
WORDS DANCE PUBLISHING

LOVE AND OTHER SMALL WARS

Poetry by Donna-Marie Riley

| $12 | 76 pages | 5.5" x 8.5" | softcover |

ISBN: 978-0615931111

Love and Other Small Wars reminds us that when you come back from combat usually the most fatal of wounds are not visible. Riley's debut collection is an arsenal of deeply personal poems that embody an intensity that is truly impressive yet their hands are tender. She enlists you. She gives you camouflage & a pair of boots so you can stay the course through the minefield of her heart. You will track the lovely flow of her soft yet fierce voice through a jungle of powerful imagery on womanhood, relationships, family, grief, sexuality & love, amidst other matters. Battles with the heart aren't easily won but Riley hits every mark. You'll be relieved that you're on the same side. Much like war, you'll come back from this book changed.

"Riley's work is wise, intense, affecting, and uniquely crafted. This collection illuminates her ability to write with both a gentle hand and a bold spirit. She inspires her readers and creates an indelible need inside of them to consume more of her exceptional poetry. I could read *Love and Other Small Wars* all day long…and I did."

— **APRIL MICHELLE BRATTEN**
editor of *Up the Staircase Quarterly*

"Riley's poems are personal, lyrical and so vibrant they practically leap off the page, which also makes them terrifying at times. A beautiful debut."

— **BIANCA STEWART**

Other titles available from
WORDS DANCE PUBLISHING

Tammy Foster Brewer is the type of poet who makes me wish I could write poetry instead of novels. From motherhood to love to work, Tammy's poems highlight the extraordinary in the ordinary and leave the reader wondering how he did not notice what was underneath all along. I first heard Tammy read 'The Problem is with Semantics' months ago, and it's stayed with me ever since. Now that I've read the entire collection, I only hope I can make room to keep every one of her poems in my heart and mind tomorrow and beyond.

— NICOLE ROSS, author

NO GLASS ALLOWED
Poetry by Tammy Foster Brewer

$12 | 56 pages | 6" x 9" | softcover | ISBN: 978-0615870007

Brewer's collection is filled with uncanny details that readers will wear like the accessories of womanhood. Fishing the Chattahoochee, sideways trees, pollen on a car, white dresses and breast milk, and so much more -- all parts of a deeply intellectual pondering of what is often painful and human regarding the other halves of mothers and daughters, husbands and wives, lovers and lost lovers, children and parents.

— NICHOLAS BELARDES
author of *Songs of the Glue Machines*

Tammy deftly juxtaposes distinct imagery with stories that seem to collide in her brilliant poetic mind. Stories of transmissions and trees and the words we utter, or don't. Of floods and forgiveness, conversations and car lanes, bread and beginnings, awe and expectations, desire and leaps of faith that leave one breathless, and renewed.

"When I say I am a poet / I mean my house has many windows" has to be one of the best descriptions of what it's like to be a contemporary female poet who not only holds down a day job and raises a family, but whose mind and heart regularly file away fleeting images and ideas that might later be woven into something permanent, and perhaps even beautiful. This ability is not easily acquired. It takes effort, and time, and the type of determination only some writers, like Tammy, possess and are willing to actively exercise.

— KAREN DEGROOT CARTER
author of *One Sister's Song*

Other titles available from
WORDS DANCE PUBLISHING

Unrequited love? We've all been there.

Enter:

WHAT TO DO AFTER SHE SAYS NO
by Kris Ryan.

This skillfully designed 10-part poem explores what it's like to ache for someone. This is the book you buy yourself or a friend when you are going through a breakup or a one-sided crush, it's the perfect balance between aha, humor & heartbreak.

WHAT TO DO AFTER SHE SAYS NO
A Poem by Kris Ryan

$10 | 104 pages | 5" x 8" | softcover | ISBN: 978-0615870045

"*What to Do After She Says No* takes us from Shanghai to the interior of a refrigerator, but mostly dwells inside the injured human heart, exploring the aftermath of emotional betrayal. This poem is a compact blast of brutality, with such instructions as "Climb onto the roof and jump off. If you break your leg, you are awake. If you land without injury, pinch and twist at your arm until you wake up." Ryan's use of the imperative often leads us to a reality where pain is the only outcome, but this piece is not without tenderness, and certainly not without play, with sounds and images ricocheting off each other throughout. Anticipate the poetry you wish you knew about during your last bad breakup; this poem offers a first "foothold to climb out" from that universal experience."

— **LISA MANGINI**

"Reading Kris Ryan's *What To Do After She Says No* is like watching your heart pound outside of your chest. Both an unsettling visual experience and a hurricane of sadness and rebirth—this book demands more than just your attention, it takes a little bit of your soul, and in the end, makes everything feel whole again."

— **JOHN DORSEY**
author of *Tombstone Factory*

"*What to Do After She Says No* is exquisite. Truly, perfectly exquisite. It pulls you in on a familiar and wild ride of a heart blown open and a mind twisting in an effort to figure it all out. It's raw and vibrant...and in the same breath comforting. I want to crawl inside this book and live in a world where heartache is expressed so magnificently."

— **JO ANNA ROTHMAN**
MA, Coach & Conjurer of Electric Creative Wholeness

WORDS DANCE PUBLISHING has one aim:

To spread mind-blowing / heart-opening poetry.

Words Dance artfully & carefully wrangles words that were born to dance wildly in the heart-mind matrix. Rich, edgy, raw, emotionally-charged energy balled up & waiting to whip your eyes wild; we rally together words that were written to make your heart go boom right before they slay your mind. You dig?

Words Dance Publishing is an independent press out of Pennsylvania. We work closely & collaboratively with all of our writers to ensure that their words continue to breathe in a sound & stunning home. Most importantly though, we leave the windows in these homes unlocked so you, the reader, can crawl in & throw one fuck of a house party.

To learn more about our books, authors, events & Words Dance Poetry Magazine, visit:

WORDSDANCE.COM